Biréli Lagrène

Gypsy Jazz Guitar Artistry

 TAGA Publishing

Online Audio www.melbay.com/30729MEB

WWW. MELBAY.COM

Contents

Preface

ABOUT BIRÉLI LAGRÈNE AND THIS BOOK

We at TAGA Publishing had the tremendous honor of filming French guitar legend Biréli Lagrène, who is one of the most influential jazz guitarists of the past few decades. He has performed and recorded in a plethora of styles including Gypsy jazz, bebop, fusion, and more. Biréli has performed in front of countless audiences, filled concert halls and headlined at festivals since he was a child. He has played and performed with artists such as Benny Goodman, Stéphane Grappelli, Al Di Meola, Paco de Lucía, John McLaughlin, the Gil Evans Orchestra, Benny Carter, Jaco Pastorius, Stanley Clarke, Larry Coryell, Stanley Jordan and countless more. Discovered and regarded as a child prodigy, he stunned audiences worldwide by playing traditional Gypsy jazz style and flashy Django Reinhardt lines from a very young age.

Playing every style so unbelievably well and seemingly effortlessly, his skills and spontaneity with the instrument are simply mind blowing. Let's not forget to mention that he also plays the bass, violin, drums, and piano like a wizard, but that's a different topic for another day.

You may be asking yourself, "How is it possible that someone can reach that degree of artistry and mastery of the instrument?" Or, you might say, "There is no way that I will ever be able reach that level of performance in my lifetime! The good news is - these are all learnable skills.

In TAGA Publishing's "*Biréli Lagrène: Gypsy Jazz Guitar Artistry*" Biréli shares priceless insights to help you discover and get started in learning:

- The basic rhythms used in the Gypsy jazz style of accompaniment, and
- The "must-know vocabulary" to improvise in the Gypsy jazz style.

All of the material has been impeccably transcribed and notated both in standard notation and TAB for your practice, reference and study purposes.

This project is a dream come true for all of us here at tagapublishing.com

We can't thank Biréli enough for trusting us with the project, and we are thrilled to present to you "*Biréli Lagrène: Gypsy Jazz Guitar Artistry*".

INTERVIEW WITH BIRÉLI LAGRÈNE

[TAGA]: *When did you start playing? Approximately how old were you?*

[Biréli Lagrène]: *I must have been around four. That was my very first encounter with the guitar.*

[TAGA]: *Was it something that you just saw around the house?*

[BL]: *I don't really know because the problem is, I cannot remember very well. My mother and father told me afterwards how I picked up the guitar at first. They said I just played and played and played.*

[TAGA]: *The guitar, meanwhile, was still bigger than you were at that point...*

[BL]: *I think it was, yes! It's funny, because my mother used to tell me how I started to play the guitar. I would lay it on the floor and I just had the neck over my knees. So I would, you know, play on the neck. And the rest of the guitar was over there [on the floor].*

[TAGA]: *Did you come from a musical background, a musical family?*

[BL]: *Yes, I came from a musical background. My father used to have a band in the 40s. They would play swing stuff, you know. He was a guitar player. My mother used to play a little violin. The whole side of my father's family were musicians back in the early 1900s. Although I had friends, I really preferred to stay home playing the guitar. This is also when I began to get the first draw from other people. They came to our house. People like the mayor from the little town I used to live in came. All of a sudden I became a regional attraction. My father just was going crazy because he was loving so much that I was able to play the guitar. And obviously at a certain, good level, you know.*

[TAGA]: *I've seen videos of you playing violin and bass. Did you teach yourself all that?*

[BL]: *I kind of taught myself all these instruments, yeah. I already had a certain idea what they can do. I wanted to integrate those different instruments in my own guitar playing, to see how it works.*

[BL]: *At the age of eleven, or twelve I think, it must have been, I did my first record. I remember we had a bass player in those days, because we started to create a little band. Luckily this bass player's wife had a small record company in Germany. And this is how I actually made it to record my first record. It's called "Routes to Django".*

Afterward, I made two or three other [records] in that kind of style. And then, I don't know what happened. Something just opened up in here [points to his head], you know, and I just wanted to do my own thing somehow.

[TAGA]: *You're known for that Django-style stuff, but obviously, you've gone far beyond that with the electric stuff, the "Electric Side" album. There's actually a vocal album you did, "Blue Eyes", I think it was called?*

[BL]: *It's called "Blue Eyes", yeah.*

[TAGA]: *Is there somebody that you want to play with, or wish you could have played with, that you have not been able to yet?*

[BL]: *Forgive me if I say this, but I have to say it. It's still a dream. Miles. Miles Davis.*

[TAGA]: *Let's teach people to play like you! They should know that it takes many hours, many years. Lots of blood, sweat, and tears.*

[BL]: *Yep, yep, yep. I went through that when I was a teenager, man. I was playing almost nonstop.*

[TAGA]: *It's truly not for the weak-hearted because it takes a lifetime.*

[BL]: *And it never ends.*

On Meeting Stéphane Grappelli - The Grandfather of Jazz Violinists
(1908 - 1997)

[Biréli Lagrène]: *I went to see [Grappelli's] concert with my father and brother. That was even before I started my career, actually. I must have been nine or ten. Some Gypsy people knew him, and one of my uncles, I think, knew him. So we waited for the intermission of the concert. We all went back to the dressing room. I had my guitar with me of course, and I played a few notes. Now, he thought I would play some, you know, Christmas song.*

[TAGA]: *But that's not what you played... I guess he was impressed!*

[BL]: *He took me by the hand and I walked up on stage with him. We almost finished the second half of the concert together.*

[TAGA]: *That must have been a thrill for a kid that age!*

[BL]: *That was fun.*

A BRIEF HISTORY OF DJANGO REINHARDT AND HIS MUSIC

Django Reinhardt at the Aquarium jazz club in New York, NY, circa November 1946 (William P. Gottlieb).

Jean "Django" Reinhardt was born on January 23, 1910 in Liberchies, Pont-à-Celles, Belgium into a Belgian family. His ancestry was of Manouche Romani descent. He was the first jazz talent to emerge from Europe and remains the most significant. In addition, Django is still regarded as one of the greatest musicians of the twentieth century.

He became famous for his unique musical sound which blended elements of American jazz with traditional European and Romani music. Django's father was a musician and entertainer and his mother was a dancer. Being that his family were Manouches, they were nomadic. However, they eventually settled in a camp near Paris. Raised without any formal schooling, Reinhardt was practically illiterate.

As a child, Django learned to play the banjo-guitar, a hybrid of a guitar and banjo. He was self-taught and never learned to read or write music. By his early teens he was already playing in clubs in Paris. Reinhardt started out playing popular French music, but became interested in American jazz in the mid-1920s. He especially liked the works of Duke Ellington and Louis Armstrong. His promising career, however, was almost ended by a terrible caravan fire accident in 1928 which left him with his ring and pinky fingers paralyzed.

In 1934, he formed the Paris-based Quintette du Hot Club de France in 1934 with violinist Stéphane Grappelli. They were among the first to play jazz that featured the guitar as a lead instrument. Django also recorded in France with many visiting American musicians, including Benny Carter and Coleman Hawkins. He also briefly toured the United States with Duke Ellington's orchestra in 1946.

Some of Django Reinhardt's most popular compositions have become jazz standards. These include songs such as "Minor Swing," "Daphne," "Djangology," and "Nuages." Over the last few decades, annual Django festivals have been held throughout the world. In addition, several biographies have been written about his life, and a movie entitled "Django" [in French with English subtitles] was made about him in 2017.

He died suddenly of a stroke at the age of 43.

DJANGO REINHARDT-STYLE
RHYTHM EXAMPLES

The following examples are typical of how a Gypsy jazz guitarist would play chords to accompany other musicians. In Gypsy jazz, the role of the right hand is crucial in determining the rhythmic feel ("la pompe"). Getting this feel right is largely a question of experience, so be sure to listen to and watch as much Gypsy jazz as possible.

Example 1

To get started, and help get the right feel, begin by just playing one chord per beat. Play each chord with a downstroke. Importantly, notice that the chords on beats 2 and 4 are played staccato.

This example also shows how passing diminished chords can be used in Gypsy jazz. Notice the resulting strong bass motion. This smooth, chromatic bass line is especially effective if you find yourself playing in an ensemble without a bass player. In this example the left hand often plays "shell" voicings, meaning that some chord tones can be omitted. Notice, for example, how in the Am6 chord, the 5th (E) is left out. Interestingly, this means we can use exactly the same left-hand shape for the diminished seventh chords and the minor 6 chords.

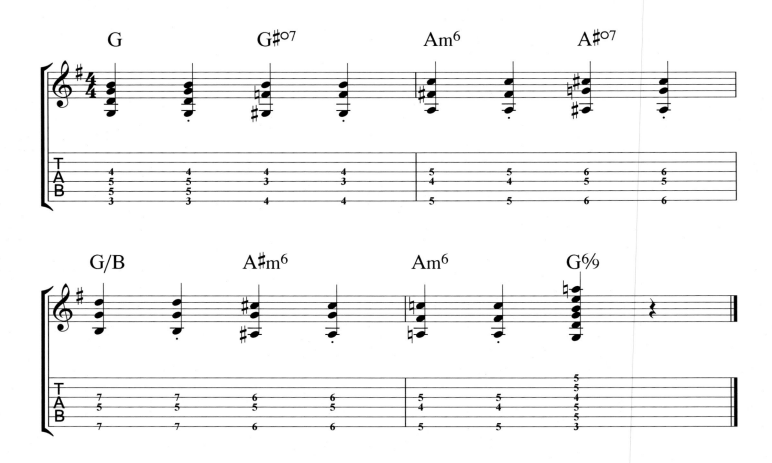

Example 2

Harmonically, this example is similar to the previous one. Notice however, in bar 4 the use of eighth notes and syncopation.

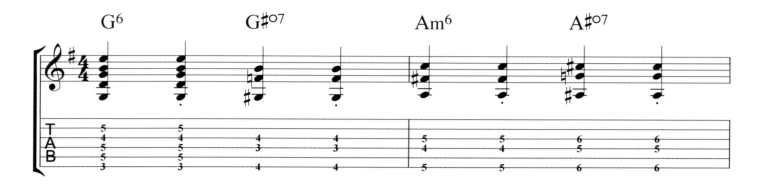

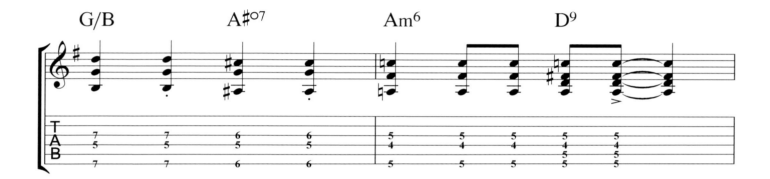

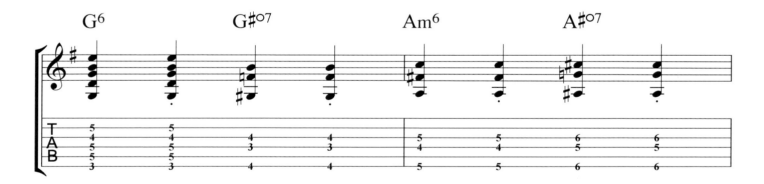

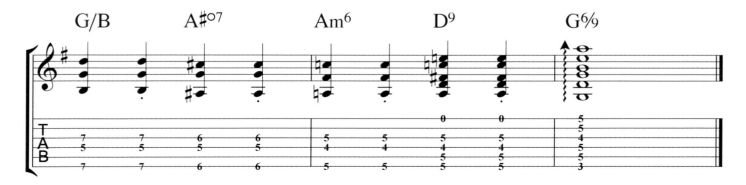

9

Example 3

Let's go back to the basic quarter-note rhythm. This example employs larger, 5-note voicings on string group 6 through 2.

Staccato is even more prominent in this example. This is achieved by gently releasing the pressure in the fretting hand immediately after each stroke. This "bouncing" motion is essential to capturing the spirit of Gypsy jazz.

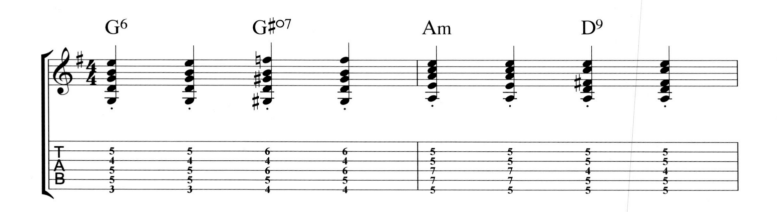

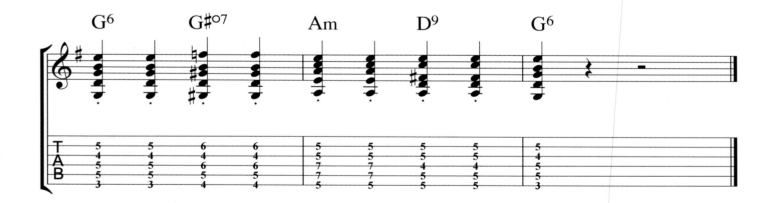

Example 4

Sometimes you may wish to vary the texture of your accompaniment by playing only a bass note on beats 1 and 3, and a chord on beats 2 and 4 as shown throughout this example.

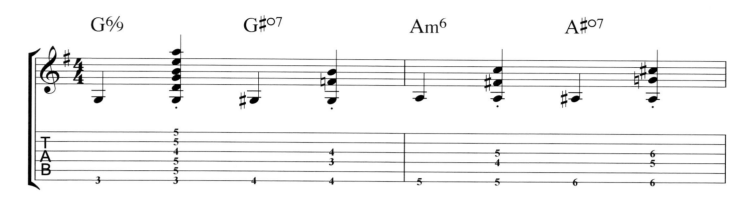

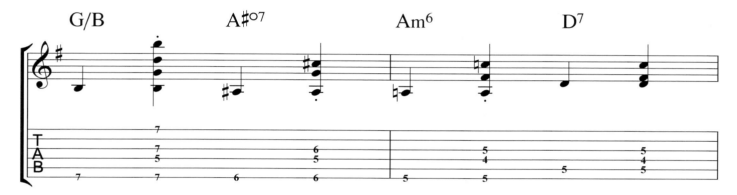

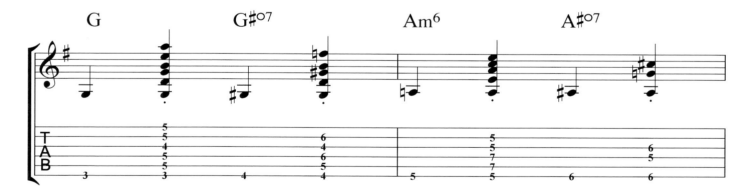

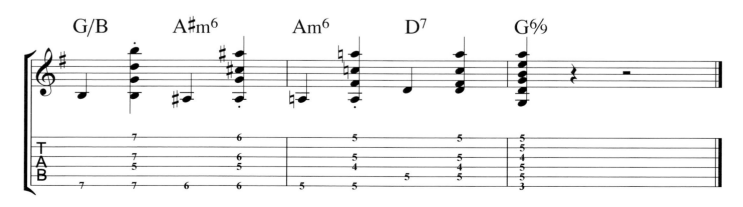

Example 5

This example showcases some other voicings that can be used when playing Gypsy jazz rhythm guitar. Many chords are not in root position. Notice how this allows us to play a bass line that descends chromatically in bars 3 to 6. Using single note lines in the bass (as in the last bar of lines 2 and 3) can also be a very effective way to vary the texture, as well as providing rhythmic interest. As the Gypsy jazz style is extremely rhythmic, it is natural to occasionally include some percussive elements to help to drive the music forward. These are indicated with an "x" in the notation.

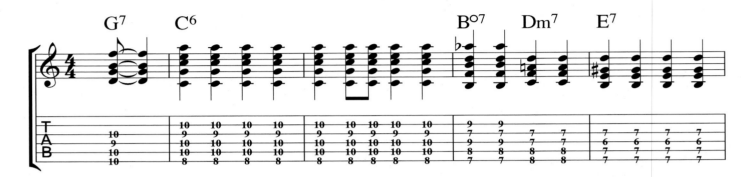

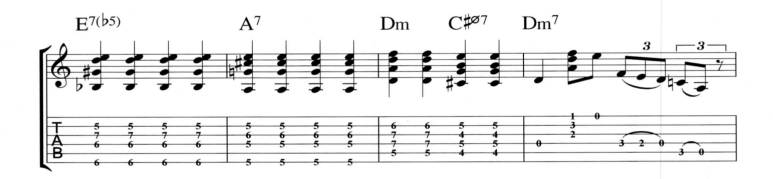

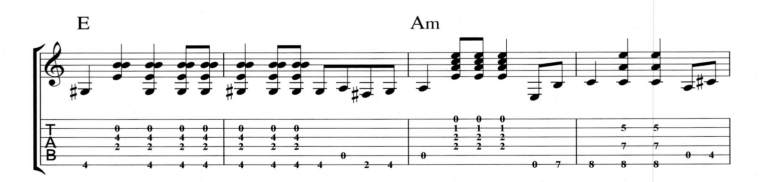

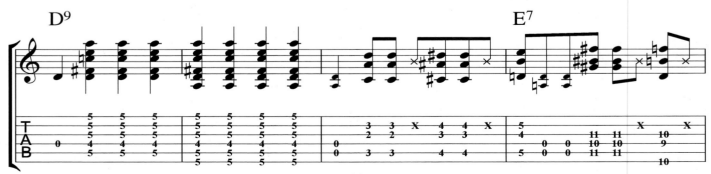

12

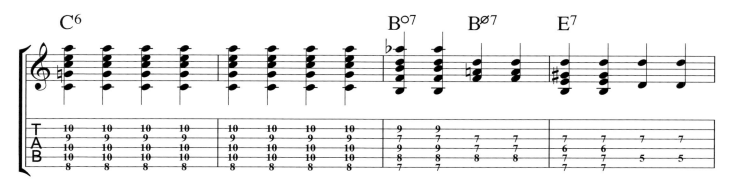

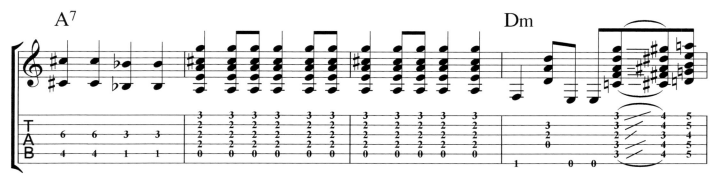

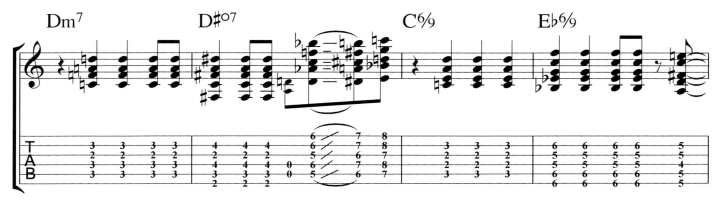

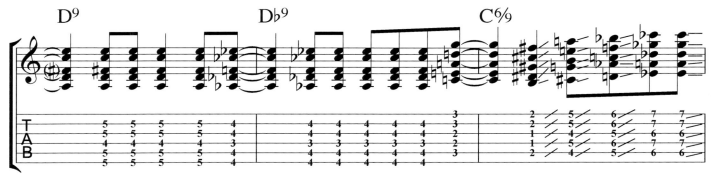

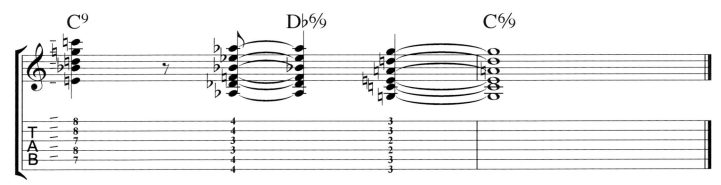

13

Example 6

This example is reminiscent of big band music. Notice how you can take a single chord shape (starting in bar 1) and move it chromatically towards a target chord (the chord at the beginning of bar 2). The staccato chords in bars 3 and 4 evoke the "shouts" that are characteristic of much big band music.

Django Reinhardt and Duke Ellington, Aquarium, New York, N.Y.,
ca. November 1946 (William P. Gottlieb).

Biréli Lagrène, Jazzfestival St. Ingbert, Germany, 2015

ON PLAYING BY EAR

I wanted to learn how to read and write music, of course. But I never had the chance because people would say "Man, Biréli, you play so well, you don't need to read. I mean, look how fast it goes. You hear a melody once and you can pick it up, it's no problem."

The thing is, if you have to learn somebody else's music, of course, it will take you a little longer than if you were a very good sight reader.

Of course, I have nothing against people who read. I think it's a great thing.

Example 7

Here is a demonstration of a completely different accompaniment style for Gypsy jazz, the Bolero. If you want to play this rhythm correctly, it is imperative to follow the order of the strokes. Notice we have two downstrokes, followed by one upstroke, then two more downstrokes before ending with the final four downstrokes.

$(\vee)$ = upstroke

(Π) = downstroke

Example 8 - Troublant Boléro - Right Hand

Let's apply the strumming pattern we've just studied to part of the chord progression for "Troublant Boléro" by Django Reinhardt.

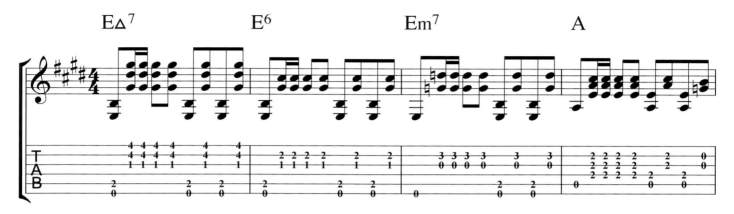

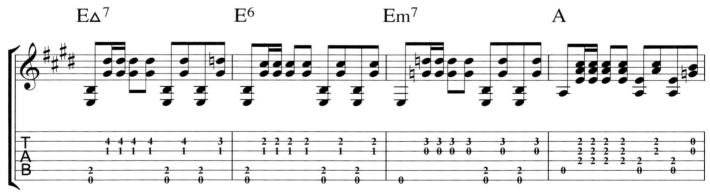

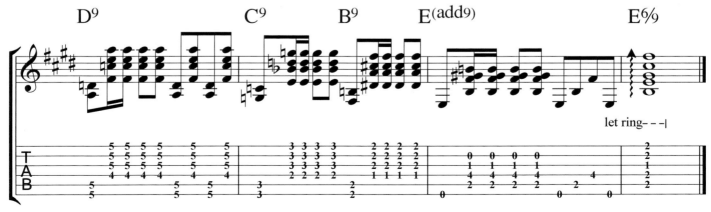

DJANGO REINHARDT-STYLE LINES

Example 9

This "Django-style" lick uses unison notes on adjacent strings with a repeating down-up-up strumming pattern. This strumming pattern goes against the beat and creates an interesting sense of syncopation. Notice how each bar starts with a slur from the fret below. This, and the down-up-up strumming, give the whole phrase a biting, aggressive quality.

($\lor$) = upstroke

($\sqcap$) = downstroke

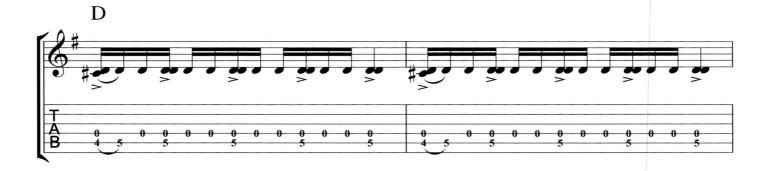

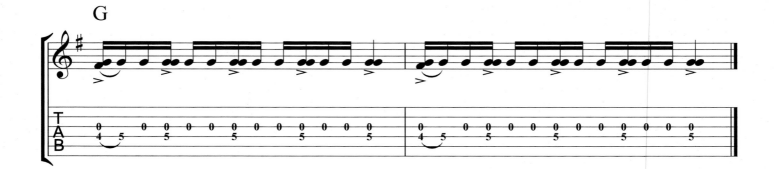

Example 10

This example shows the tremolo technique (rapid alternate picking on one string) with the right hand and descends through a sequence of falling fourths in G Major. Here, we cover the span of an octave, starting on the guitar's highest B and finishing on the B at the seventh fret of the high E string. The most difficult part of this example is keeping your right hand tremolo consistent while sliding in and out of the correct frets. Try adapting this lick so that, instead of starting and ending on the third degree of the scale, you start and end on other degrees. You should also try applying this idea to other scales.

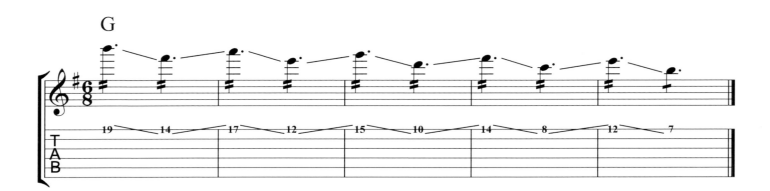

JUST GO FOR IT

I'm from that era where all the guitar players just grew up out of the ground. There were so many of them.

I didn't ask myself, "Well, should I do it?" I just did it.

Biréli Lagrène Gypsy Project, Gouvy Jazz & Blues Festival, Belgium 2008

Example 11

This phrase uses notes from the E harmonic minor scale. Notice how the first two four-note cells are the same, just in a different octave. This is a good example of how to cover a large range on the instrument in a short amount of time, climbing through three octaves in the span of just one measure.

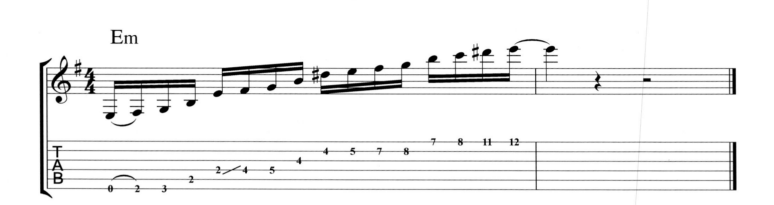

Example 12

Here's a very versatile idea using diatonic major and minor thirds in eighth-note triplets. It is played in the key of C on just the highest two strings. This four-bar phrase ends with a minor sixth interval played on beat 2 of the last measure.

Apply the picking pattern suggested in bar 1 throughout this example.

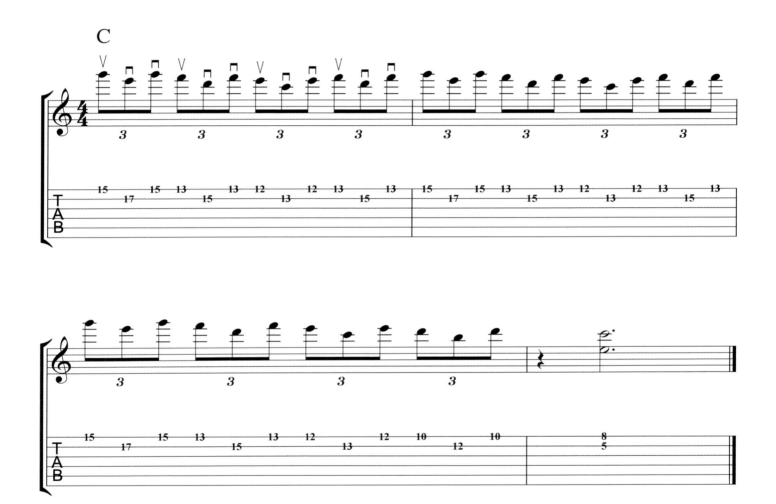

Example 13

This example effectively utilizes two simple ideas: The first being a chromatically descending melody (beat 1 of bars 1 through 5); the second consisting of ascending arpeggios to outline each chord. This is counterbalanced by a descending ii-V-I phrase in measures 5 through 8.

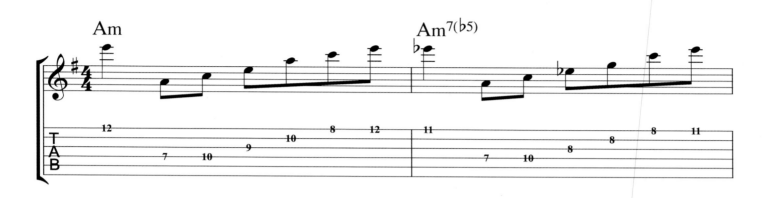

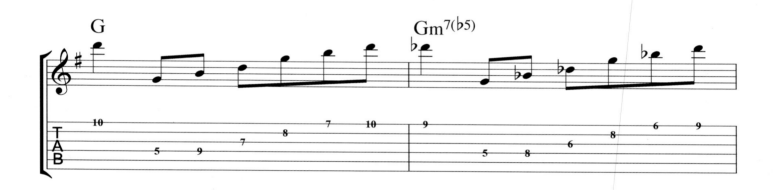

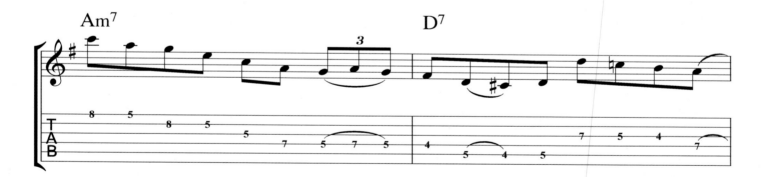

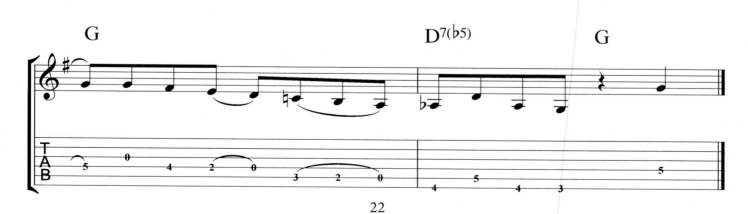

Example 14

As with all of the phrases in this book, you are encouraged to permutate them with simple alterations such as rests, ornaments and rhythmic displacement. To illustrate, compare measures 5 through 8 of this example with the same measures of Example 13.

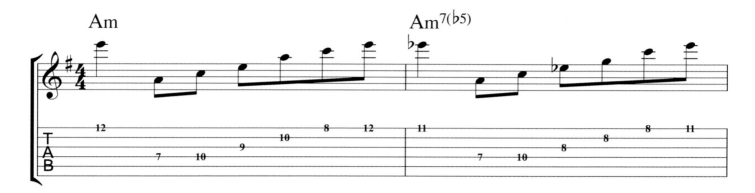

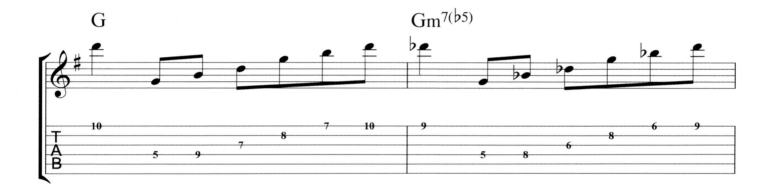

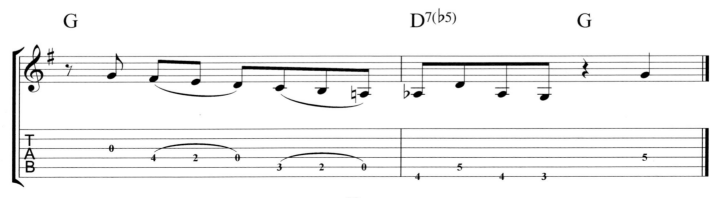

Example 15

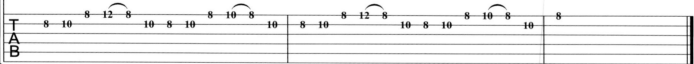

This example is a major pentatonic idea that features pull-offs in a repeating triplet figure. Notice how the first group of six notes differs from the second group by just one note. Apply the picking pattern suggested in measure 1 throughout this example.

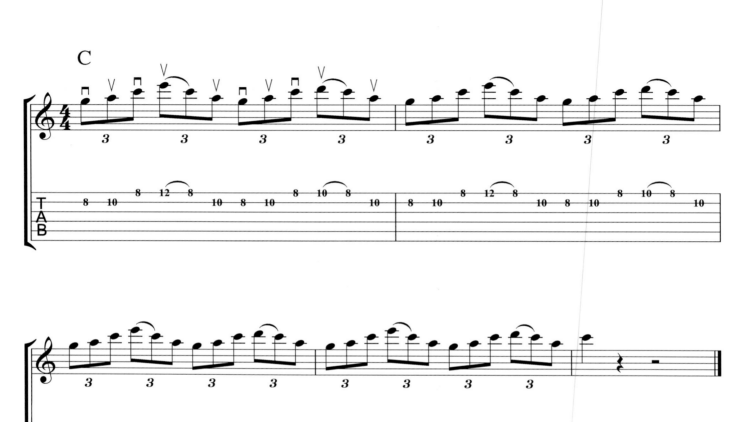

Example 16

This 32nd-note phrase is very reminiscent of one of Django Reinhardt's favorite techniques. It starts off with what is very close to a chromatic scale. Once you reach the open E string (1st string) in the second half of the first bar, you should slide up the first string while picking every note. This impressive technique is difficult to do in time. Rather than merely approximating this effect, work on synchronizing the left and right hands.

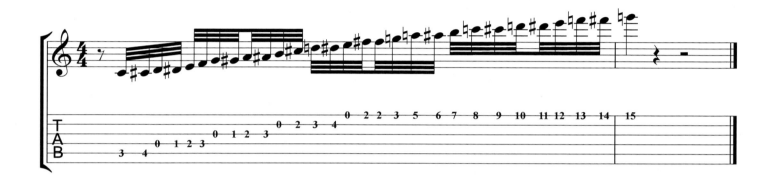

Biréli Lagrène, Festival des Granges, Laimont, France, 2006

I'm a music servant.
That's probably the best expression concerning myself.

Example 17

This phrase illustrates how fast chromatic runs such as the one we learned in the previous example can be applied in context. Measure 1 consists of the root (C) and the 5th (G) connected by scalar motion. Notice how this both sets up and creates an effective contrast to the virtuosic scale that follows.

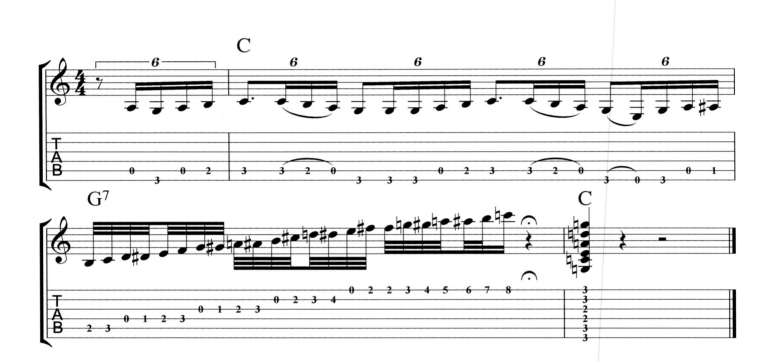

LICKS BASED ON FINGER PATTERNS

Example 18

This example is a symmetrical phrase that can be used over any dominant chord. It starts with your index finger (1st finger) on the 4th fret of the 4th string and goes all the way up to the first string before descending in the same fashion.

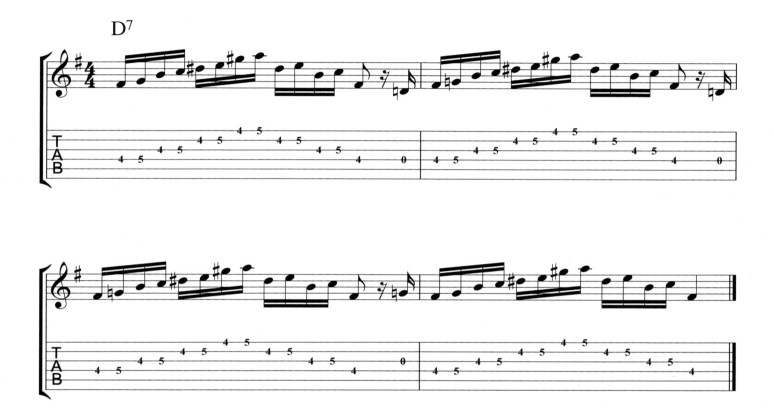

Example 19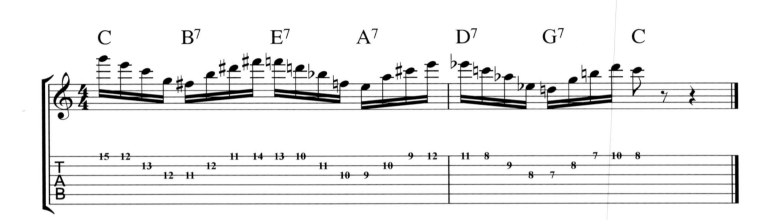

This example is a two-bar phrase utilizing a four-note major arpeggio. It shows how much can be done with just a simple motif such as this. After the descending arpeggio, it ascends, but a semitone lower. The next descent is a semitone lower again, and this pattern is repeated until we arrive at the tonic, C. Try seeing what else you can do with similar four-note motifs.

Biréli Lagrène, Strasbourg, France 2017

I don't like to overplay myself on a day when I feel like practicing.
Just an hour is okay, you know?

Example 20

The finger pattern used here, when shifted by one fret, outlines passing chords (Gm6 and Ddim7) which add tension to a line that would otherwise be harmonically static. Each arpeggio starts on the open D string and uses the same pattern and fingering. Once you've executed the first sextuplet group, you can simply move your fingers up a fret for the next group and use the same finger pattern.

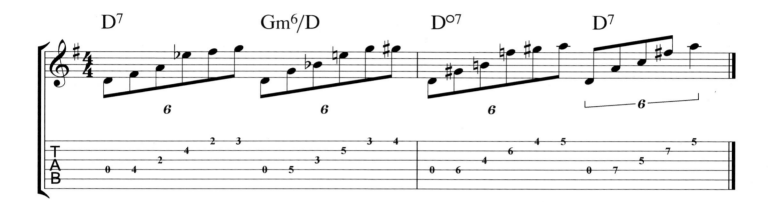

29

NEIGHBOR-NOTE LICKS

Example 21

This two-octave phrase outlines a D major triad with neighboring tones and chromaticism. This very common pattern consists of the following four-note cell:

1. Diatonic upper neighbor note
2. Target note
3. Chromatic lower neighbor note
4. Target note

Notice that the target notes are always the root, 3rd or 5th of the chord. So in this example in D Major, you'll want to aim for D, F♯ and A. As with other examples, to get the most out of this idea, be sure to transpose it to different keys (see Example 23) and apply it to different chord types (see Example 22). You could even change the order of the notes in the cell.

Example 22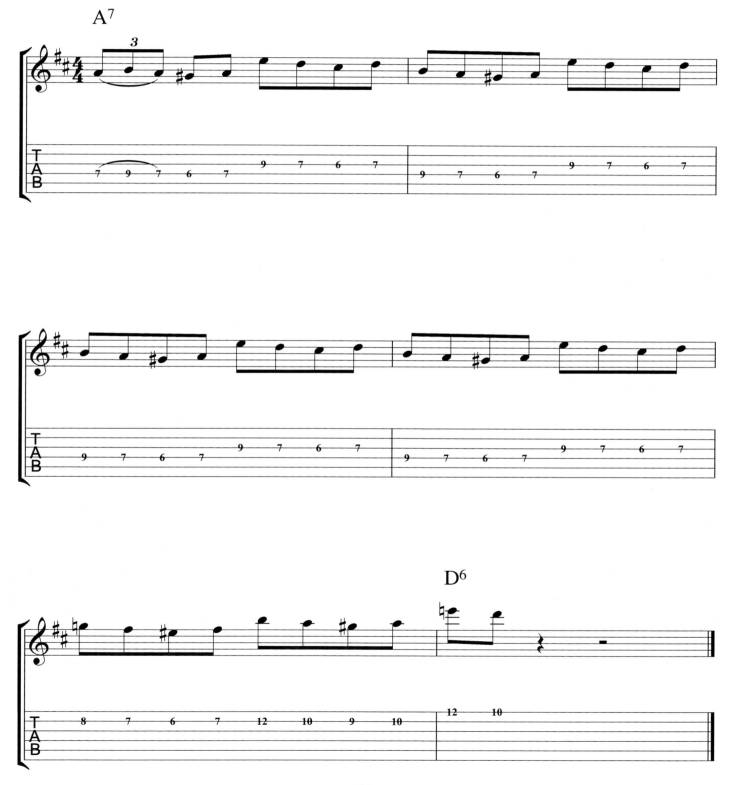

This example also uses a repeating upper and lower neighboring tone motif. It's similar to Example 21 in that it also employs an upper neighbor note and a lower chromatic neighbor note. However, this lick creates a sense of insistence by repeating the same idea four times, rather than moving the cells through an arpeggio, as happens in the previous example.

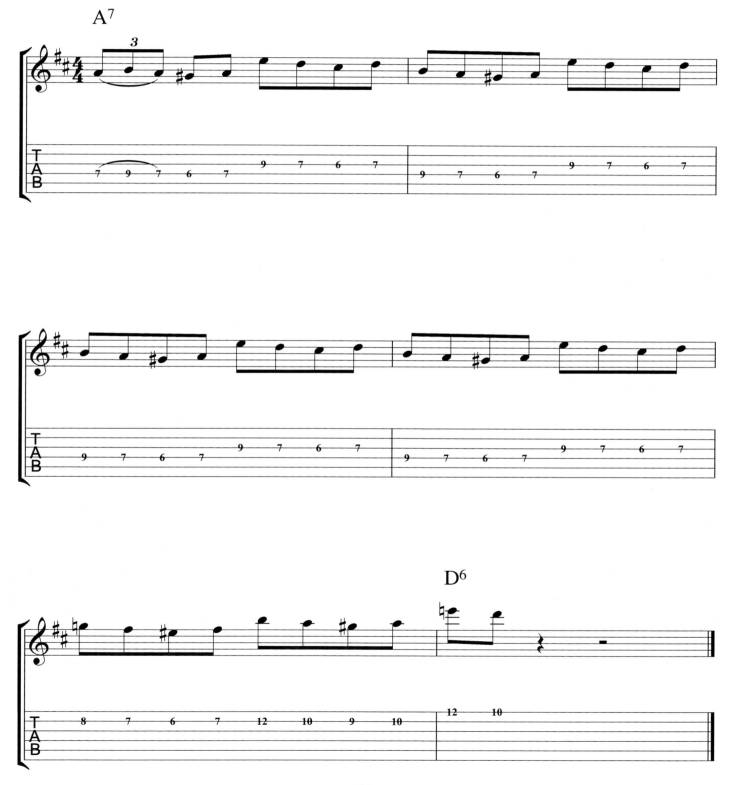

Example 23

As with the other neighboring note licks, the upper note is diatonic while the lower note is chromatic. This example is played in the key of G major. Again, to thoroughly master the Gypsy jazz vocabulary presented in this book, be sure to transpose each phrase to various keys. That way, these phrases will become a natural part of your repertoire.

DIMINISHED ARPEGGIO LICKS

Example 24

This first example can be thought about in two ways. The first way is as a simple diminished 7th arpeggio. Since the diminished chord/scale/arpeggio can be called by 4 different names, it can either be called an F♯ (G♭) diminished 7th, A diminished 7th, C diminished 7th, or E♭ diminished 7th. The second way to look at this line is to think of it as a D7♭9 arpeggio starting from the 3rd. Therefore, as you can see, the notes are F♯ (3rd), A (5th), C (7th), and E♭ (♭9) and are played in two octaves.

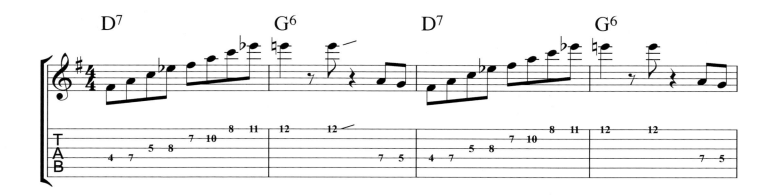

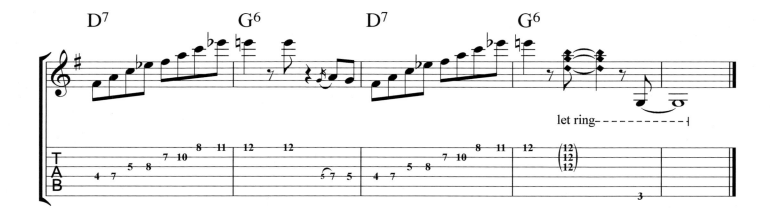

Example 25

Here is a diminished lick covering the the top three strings of the guitar. It can be used over many different dominant 7th or diminished chords (see Example 24). It starts on the 7th of E7 and outlines a D diminished seventh arpeggio.

The 7th (D) and 5th (B) of the E7 chord are connected chromatically with a descending slur (see start of measure 2).

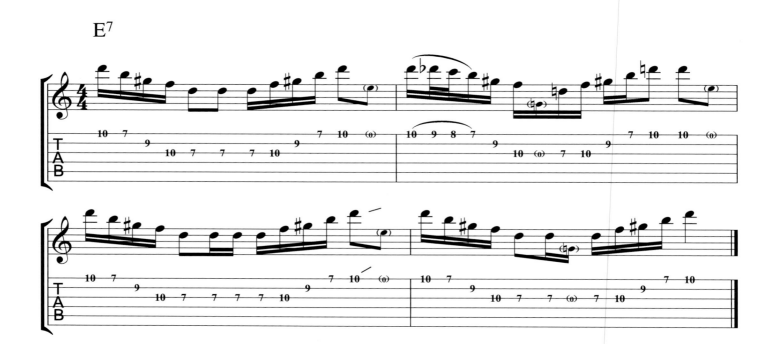

Example 26

The first two bars of this example are a *sequence* and are based around diminished seventh arpeggios. The interesting aspect of this phrase is that the position shifts do not happen on the beat.

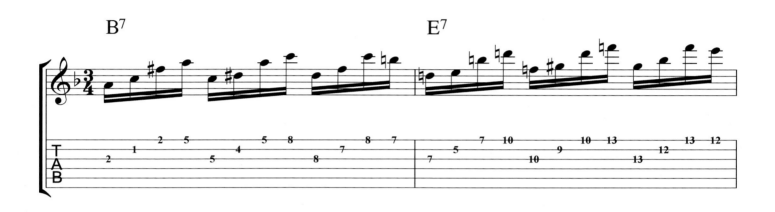

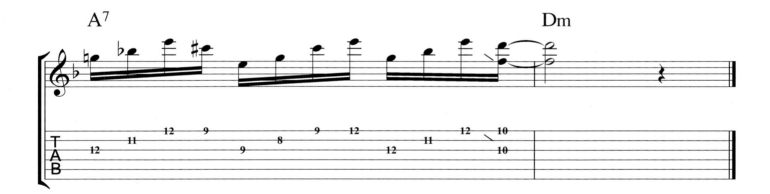

Example 27

This phrase is similar to the previous one. It is in a different key, played in 4/4 and resolved on a major chord. Once again, the position shifts don't happen on the beat.

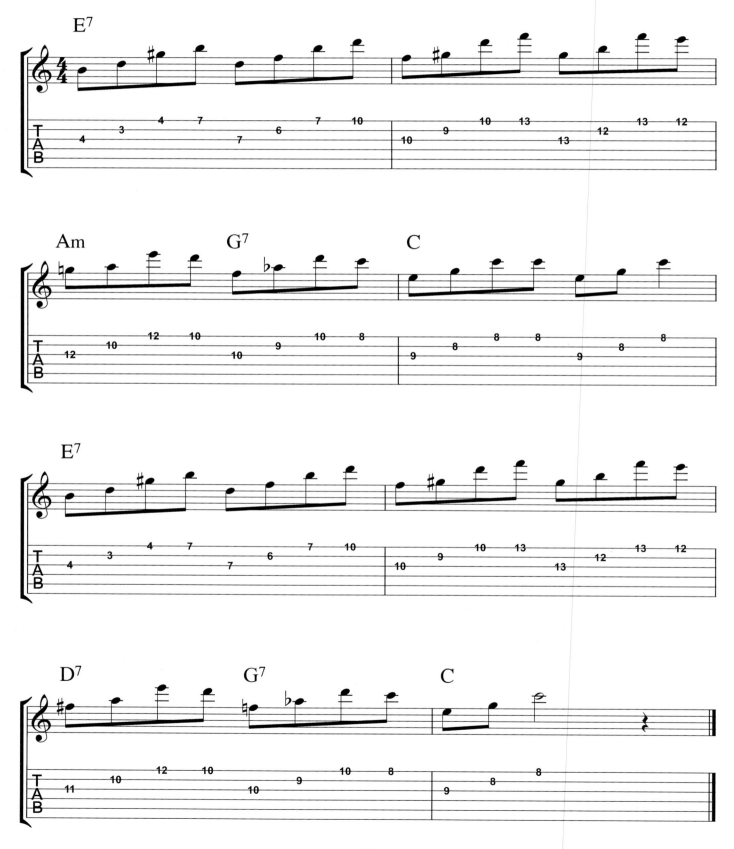

OTHER ARPEGGIO LICKS

Example 28

This next phrase is basically an A minor triad played across the fretboard in three octaves. However, the following three examples show how a simple idea can be varied and embellished in various ways in order to add interest.

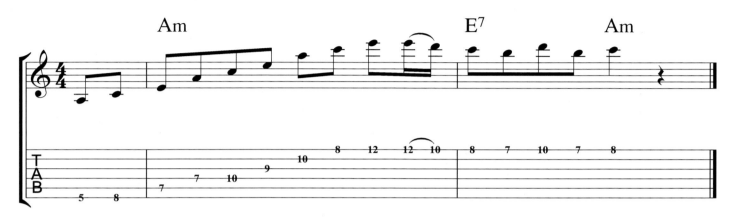

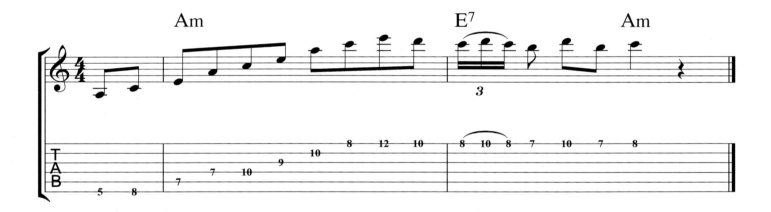

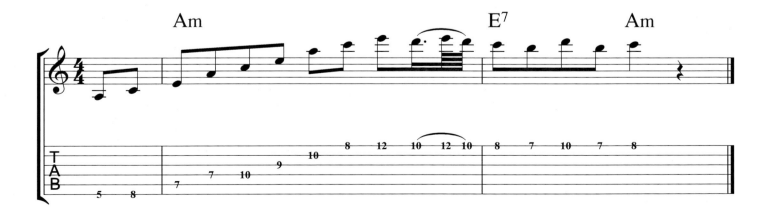

Example 29

This phrase uses a C major arpeggio starting on the 5th (G) followed by a sequence of appoggiaturas (the F♯s to Gs) in 4 different octaves. Notice how the F♯s add color.

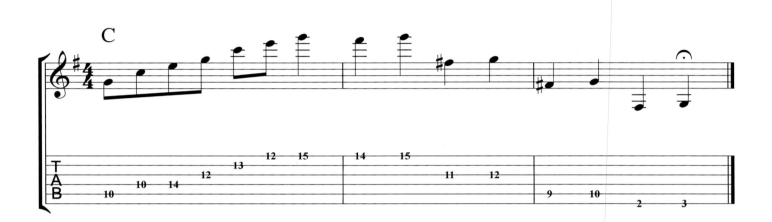

Selmer-Maccaferri jazz guitar by luthier Hanno Kiel

Example 30

This phrase is used over a ii-V7 chord progression in the key of A Major. In measure one, the first two chord tones (B and D) are connected by chromaticism. (Notice the similarity in this respect with Exercise 25). Then, as in the neighbor-note licks section, we use diatonic and chromatic neighboring notes to approach a target note (the first B of measure 2). However, in this example we have:

1. Chromatic lower neighbor note (last note of bar 1 - A♯)
2. Diatonic upper neighbor note (first note of bar 2 - C♯)
3. Target note (B)

Following this, we descend down a Bm7 arpeggio before playing a triplet and landing on the major 3rd (G♯) of the V chord (E7) at the beginning of the third bar to emphasize the sound of E7. In addition, notice the use of slurs in this example.

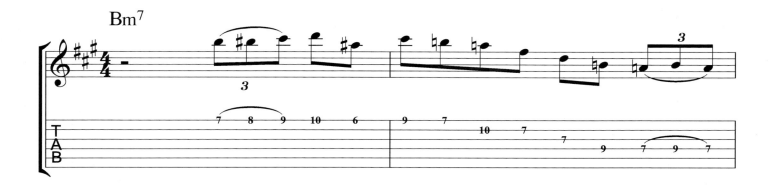

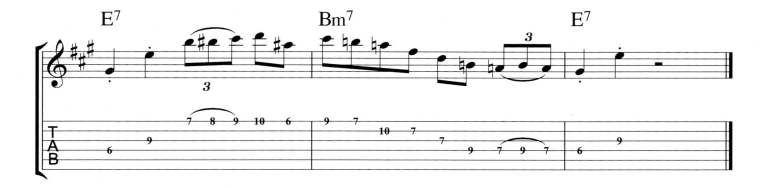

Creating Your Own Licks 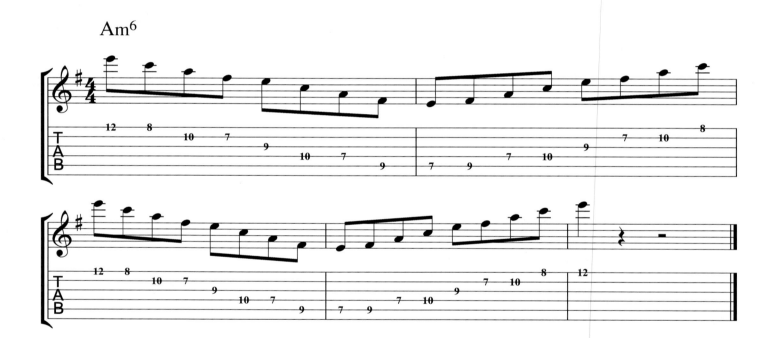 31 a

Consider the following four examples as a set. Compare them and notice how by
making even just a small change, you can create completely fresh sounding licks.
After studying these four examples, continue to experiment with them to create your
own Gypsy jazz lines.

Example 31a

The first phrase of this example spells out the chord tones of an Am6 chord (A, C, E,
and F♯). Notice how important the 6th (F♯) is to the phrase. The 6th in general is a
very important sound and is a big part of the jazz language. Saxophone legend
Lester Young loved using the 6th and did so all the time.

Example 31b b

In the last beat of this one-bar phrase, we skip the 6th (F♯) and go from the 5th (E) to the root (A). This gives us room for an extra note (D♯) at the end of the phrase, which leads chromatically back to the beginning of the phrase. Adding chromatic neighbor notes like this is a good way to add interest to licks.

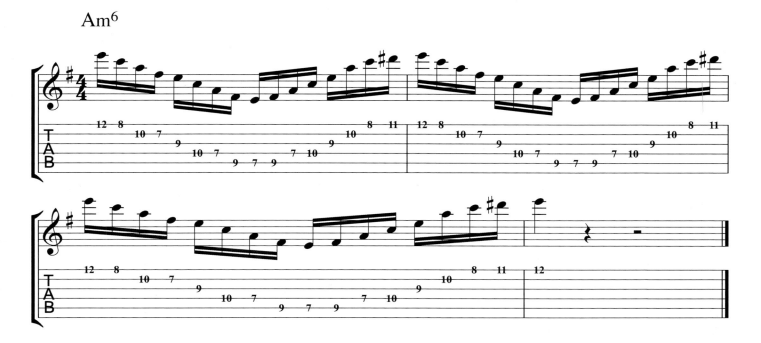

Example 31c c

Comparing this example with Example 31a we see that both licks use basically the same arpeggio. In this example, however, the arpeggio is rhythmically displaced, or shifted back by an eighth note. This means that the C (the second note of Example 31a) now falls on a downbeat. Starting with an upbeat is another way to easily vary a phrase.

Example 31d   d

The pitches in this lick are identical to the those used in Example 31c. Only the rhythms are different. Interest is added through the use of triplets.

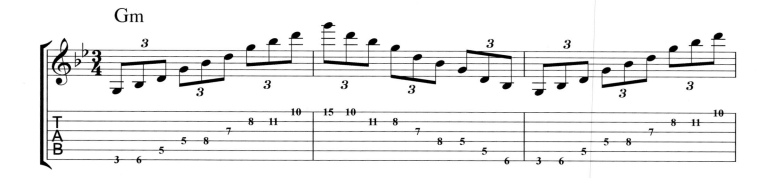

Example 32

This phrase is simply a G minor arpeggio played ascending and descending in triplets. While the idea might be simple, the challenge lies in executing this lick cleanly and with panache. The large range (three octaves) makes this an impressive-sounding lick to add to your arsenal.

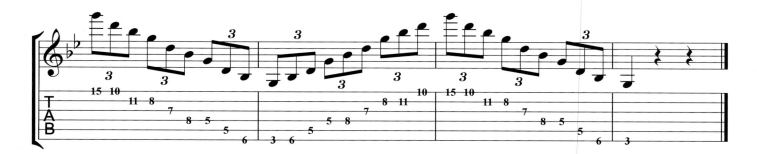

Example 33

This lick consists of the same phrase played four times. Don't be afraid of using repetition in your playing. This phrase is essentially an ascending E9 arpeggio (E, G, B, D, F♯) starting on the 3rd (G♯) and ending on the 9th degree (F♯). Ascending licks such as these are common in Gypsy jazz and have a confident, assertive quality – perfect for the style.

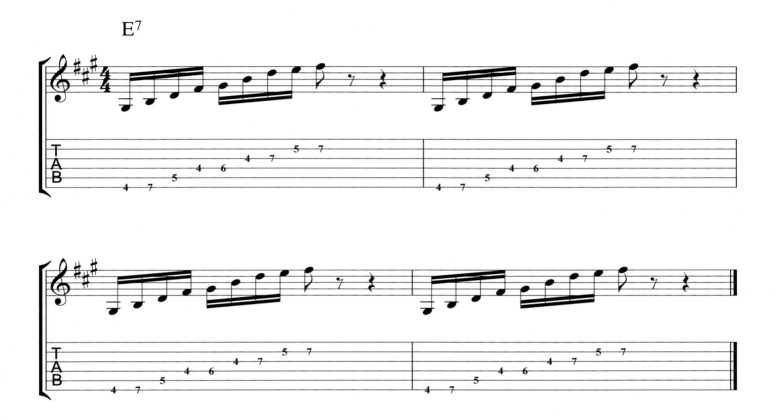

And there we go again,
the famous words:
"practice, practice."
Not too much practice..
Practice what is needed, but practice.
I wish you good luck.

Biréli Lagrène

TAGA Video Courses

Biréli Lagrène, Mike Stern, Larry Coryell, Pat Martino, Jack Wilkins, Mark Whitfield, Bucky Pizzarelli and others.

tagapublishing.com

Mel Bay Gypsy Jazz Guitar Books

Backup Trax/Swing & Jazz for Guitar (Bruce)

Getting Into Gypsy Jazz Guitar (Wrembel)

Hot Club Session (Schell)

L'Espirit Manouche (Romane)

Music of Django Reinhardt (Ayeroff)

Rhythm Guitar Chord System (M. Bay)

Frank Vignola's Complete Rhythm Play-Along for Guitar

Frank Vignola's Complete Jammin' the Blues Play-Along for Guitar

Play-Along Jazz Standard Chord Progressions (Vignola)

Tommy Emmanuel/Frank Vignola: Just Between Frets

240 2-Bar Jazz Guitar Riffs (Vignola)

Comping the Blues (Vignola)

www.melbay.com